A Child Turns Back to Wave

Poetry of Lost Places

A Child Turns Back to Wave

Poetry of Lost Places

Peter Neil Carroll

THE POETRY PRESS
Hollywood, California

Published by
THE POETRY PRESS
of Press Americana

the press of

Americana:
The Institute for the Study of
American Popular Culture
7095-1240 Hollywood Boulevard
Hollywood, CA 90028

http://www.americanpopularculture.com

© 2012 Peter Neil Carroll

Cover Art: Photograph taken in Lincoln County, New Mexico by Jeannette Ferrary

Library of Congress Cataloging-in-Publication Data

Carroll, Peter N.
A child turns back to wave : poetry of lost places / Peter Neil Carroll.
p. cm.
Includes bibliographical references.
ISBN 978-0-9829558-4-0
I. Title.
PS3603.A7748C55 2012
811'.6--dc23
2012028863

Table of Contents

Part 1

Stone Heads   1
Solstice   3
Medicine Wheel, Wyoming   4
Chance   5
Horse Creek, 1846   6
A Skirmish in the Territory, 1854   7
Bugle, 1866   8
Winter Counts (*Waniyetu Wowapi*)   9
Black Hills   10
The Emigrant Express   12
Exodus   13
Prairie's Edge   15
Wild Museums   16
Little Big Horn   17
Crazy Horse Faces the Music   19
Things We Missed   20
Epitaph   21

Part 2

Rio Grande   22
Checkpoint   23
Desert   24
Hatch   25
16 de Septiembre Fiesta   26
Crossing the Black Range   28
Waiting for the Moon   29
Gila Canyon   30
Journey of the Dead   31
Trinity, New Mexico   33
Dawn   36

How The World Ends   38

Part 3

Soundings   39
Pearl Haiku   41
Panama Hotel, Seattle   43
Tule Lake   44
Loss   47
Confinement   48

Part 4

Contact   49
Fort Ross   50
Our Silence   51
Restless Spring   52
Redwood   53
This Curve of Earth   54
Underground   55
After the Storm   56
The Window   57
Winter Light   58

Part 5

Appalachia   59
Ponds   60
Wheeling, Dealing   61
The Puzzle   63
City on a Hill   64
The Mountain Top   65
Twenty-Nine Dead   67
Small Business   68

Hidden Valley   69
Names   70
Everlasting   72
Trespass   73
Off the River   74
Illinois Central   75

Endnotes   76

Acknowledgments   78

About the Author   79

"Why should not we also enjoy
an original relation to the universe?"
R.W. Emerson, *Nature* (1836)

For Jeannette

PART 1

Stone Heads

Too bad Jim wasn't born
back in the day when phrenology
ruled the halls of science. No doubt
Harvard experts would have read
the little bumps on the north side
of his cranium to explain
how rocks shape imagination.

Once we were drinking beer
in a tavern near Mt. Monadnock.
Jim says out of the blue,
Did you ever see Stonehenge?

Well, I started thinking, when
driving through Connecticut, I noticed
how stones gated the roads,
cluttered the nutmeg fields.
I keep those pictures inside
my brain—silence inspires Jim.

*I hear there's something like that
out in Wyoming*, he says.
Time for us to go west, I think.
Jim reads my mind perfectly,
though it takes a while for the bumps
to line up—to find maps,
translate directions
into plain English.

We're still on speaking terms
when we reach that ring of rocks
in Wyoming, give thanks
for safe passage. It's not every day
you see stone clocks
on top of the world
announcing tomorrow
is the summer solstice.

Solstice

On the high peak, white rocks speak
to the humans, but only at night when
the stars tell the rocks what to say,
and only in the summer, after the sun
releases the snow from the grass meadow
on which the rocks have been sleeping.

Then the rocks call to the dark sky,
asking the flakes of light for wisdom,
where to stand or lie down, how to form
a line that will help the rocks see clearly
and inform the waiting humans exactly
which night comes before the longest day.

Stupid men sometimes grow impatient,
scrape, kick, push the rocks along
as if bluster and strength would speed
the pace of time. Eventually even
the foolish ones laugh at their absurdity,
though strewn rocks remain as they fell.
I have picked one up, held it to my ear.

Medicine Wheel, Wyoming

What else could they do in deep darkness
but study the stars, stitch light into stories?

The holy ones spurning food and sleep
step into trance to seek prophecy or luck.

The same lure brings saints and fools
to kneel at the rim, tie gifts to the wire—

herb pouches, bundles of sticks sewn
in purple string, feathered arrows.

A buffalo skull leans on a ring of stones.
Cloudless, blue simmering light pours

as if liquid. The eyes fill with tears.
In time the wind shreds every prayer.

In stillness, the body locates its fear—
being turned, falling from the planet.

A hawk hangs, circling, wings dizzying.
I look down to see sun mirrored on a stone,

lift the red, iridescent jewel, warm in hand,
place it on a white rock—afraid to say why.

Chance

Opportunists, optimists—grains of sand
wedged in crevices, pollen pursuing
a niche. Long Ponderosa pine roots
on a narrow ledge; wind flowers dance
near the runnels. The grass yellows
to white, gray thistle sinks its teeth.

Along languid hills of Crow country, sirens
suddenly scream, two police cars going 90;
when we catch up, there's the motorcycle
that missed a curve, rumpled
on the median a brown blanket.

Instant death or slow survival, who counts
the odds of a skidding tire? A slippery hill
bringing down life petrifies what remains.
I hear a language is lost every day; every day
a species stops. Only inert earth stays,
rock and gas giving the living chance.

Horse Creek, 1846

Laughing Lakota girls and boys
splash in the cool waters,
scream with delight.

A nearly naked man holds
a white horse by a loose cord,
fixes his gaze on the procession
of canvas-covered wagons,
slow and heavy
crossing the shallow creek.

The wheels cut into dry prairie
grass, severing the roots. As far
as the horizon, he sees the wound
harden into a wide brown trail.

A Skirmish in the Territory, 1854

High Forehead thinks it's good luck when he comes upon a lame cow,
butchers the stray animal, shares the meat with his Lakota friends.

Scattering Bear sees only trouble, mounts a horse, rides quickly
to Fort Laramie, offering a gift of his horse to cover the slain cow.

The soldiers refuse to make the trade, insist on teaching the hunters
rules of property. They send a company to arrest High Forehead.

In the showdown a soldier shoots a Lakota. Then Man Afraid
of His Horse yells: *they killed one man and might be satisfied.*

But a second soldier fires his weapon. Six Lakota shoot back,
causing the blue coats to open a volley, killing five more Lakota.

The warriors pour forward, kill the lieutenant and five soldiers,
chase the fleeing men until all of them perish. And so a war.

Bugle, 1866

The bugle's beaten flat as a pancake
but how it pealed the battle cry,
ringing eighty horse soldiers into the arms
of ambush. All arrows and bullets
until bullets ran out and
Adolph gripped the bugle's shank,
a dozen wounds in his body,
swung and swung, a drummer
beating back club, fist, knife,
the last to fall at Fetterman's Fight,
then covered by Lakota warriors
with a buffalo robe, unmutilated,
to dignify an unarmed man's
uncrushed courage.

Winter Counts (*Waniyetu Wowapi*)

From first snow to first snow
Winter Counts tell stories
in pictures painted on hides.

1865-66 Lost to starvation many horses
1866-67 White man hundred they killed them
1867-68 Many flags peace men give away

Treaties signed, gold found in Black Hills,
the yellow metal that makes white men crazy,
the blue line drawn on a stomach shows hunger.

1873-74 Stricken people measles in winter
1874-75 Oglala Lakota axe U.S. flagpole
1875-76 Red Cloud's horses soldiers take away

Where the snow doesn't fall, speak written words:
Rotten food rations accuses Red Cloud in Washington;
Says the telegram: Custer's cavalry destroyed.

They were chasing us now because we remembered
and they forgot…and we were not happy any more.
I did not know then how much was ended.

1877-78 Crazy Horse they killed him
1882-83 Spotted Tail they killed him
1890-91 Big Foot they killed him

Black Hills

> "All mortal greatness is but disease."
> Herman Melville, *Moby-Dick* (1851)

1

Before coyote's howl, before the buffalo
moan; before aspen, pine, cottonwood
rustled the wind; before the black forest
in the distance played feather songs—
first came the rumble of falling waters.

Springs feed pink-finned chub; woods
hide bear, elk, deer. Patches of forget-me-nots
lie like blue carpet torn from the sky.

Through the musk of damp earth,
waterfalls still veil steep red rock,
squirrels in pairs chase under brown brush,
yellow-throats skim over shallows—

until in midstream giggly voices rise,
pony-tailed girls testing slippery rock,

> *put your right foot in,*
> *put your right foot out,*
> *do the hokey-pokey...*

Laughter of morning, bodies awakening,
their exuberance disturbs an old man's solitude:
so what, I admit.

2

Bruised bark of every frail aspen
carries the heart of Tom, DK, or Chickie,
each enchanted with Myra, Sam, or Blossom
and one anonymous, grieving girl has
engraved a two-tree sonnet to her Joey
apologizing for being drunk last night.

Graffiti, least of sins, next to stripped forest
once dark as moonless night, where lovers
of the sacred circles from birth to death
to birth became spoils of war.

3

The billboard honors the genius of desecration,
chiseler of Rushmore's faces—thumbing presidential
noses at Lakota chiefs who said the Black Hills
weren't for sale. Come visit the Wild West.
Crazy Horse Mountain Helicopter Tours. Pay here.

*HIS LEGEND WILL ENRICH YOUR PATRIOTISM**

4

Two exiled buffalo bend on a low crest,
the falling sun tints their hides, blue flies
circle around woolly ears. The dry wind
sways through sage, long yellow grass,
shimmering butterflies.

A single cloud throws a momentary shadow,
flash of dark stopping my thoughts,
of romance, rage, undoing loss.

The Emigrant Express

What if we take a fly for a ride in a rented Chevy sedan,
start in Rapid City under a gray sky, stop for scrambled
eggs at the edge of town, return to find the side-eyed gal
at the wheel reading the odometer?

We drive past a row of used cars, the airport, rolling hills.
Her little wings drift away politely, not wishing to disturb
our conversation. The sun climbs slowly, beats
the glass, we switch on cool air, she comes up front, friendly
in her way, ducks a flaying hand, nestles out of sight, uninterested
in talk of uprooted immigrants, refugees, exile.

Grazing buffalo on a hill stir a mild hum; sweating hides
I suppose equivalent to pastry in a bakery window.

The craggy-gray Badlands loom, we pause for the view,
leave the motor running, doors wide, stare at ashy rock—
desolation framed by faraway yellow hills—and leave fast
past dusty fields, clusters of cottonwood where creeks flow.

Three loud blings announce the gas tank's near empty—astonish
our fly, smarter than we thought, not taking the first chance
to escape, maybe concerned hasty departure would disturb the unborn.

Fifty miles from nowhere, over 100° outside, the fly's caught on,
excited by crisis, scoots from neck to elbow to knee, dodging blows.
Keep going, she buzzes, jumping on the mirror, not a thistle of shade.

We're hoping to make twenty miles, when a whine ruffles the air.
We look to our wispy friend, her lips showing a skimpy smile.
She dances to the windshield, paws the glass. *There*, she insists.

Green signpost: INTERIOR, POP. 67 and behind it a lone gas pump.
When we're done, we discover our passenger's gone—off to seek
her fortune, hiding under the seat, busy delivering the eggs?

Exodus

1

They're not one of Israel's Lost Tribes
as Puritans believed
but fugitives in the wilderness,
cornered on parched ground.

Their exodus is photographed
in Biblical detail:

>   Lakota chiefs sign papers
>   inside Army tents;

>   Sharp shooters destroy
>   the staples, pose
>   next to twenty-foot hills
>   of buffalo skulls;

>   Bundled men, women, children
>   huddle in lines, armed soldiers
>   keep them
>   from nailed boxes
>   of dried meat;

>   The Lakota Speckled Elk (Big Foot) lies
>   frozen on his back, arms outstretched,
>   fingers clenched where he fell
>   and was buried
>   in the blizzard at Wounded Knee.

2

Where the trail
of broken treaties stops,
mountain foliage withers
into scrabbled straw.

Maverick streams give
water to cottonwood trees;
their leaves give shade
to rusty jalopies and trailers,
topsy-turvy on yellow hills.

White crosses mark the hilltop.

Soldiers dig the long trench,
dump the frozen bodies,
nursing mothers, infants struck
while sucking, elders
running for their lives.

3

Three brown cowbirds
rise suddenly from long grass,
wing by a wood fence,
dissolve into a field
of young sunflowers.

Lizards, gray spiders
scamper for shade.
Earth's furnace
can't melt the snow
underground.

Prairie's Edge

It takes time to get lost,
the prairie ragged as the sea,
crests blur into leaden skies.

When the county road stops
at a blunt corner, we pull
into the weeds, once
someone's front yard.

An ample house leans
forward, white paint peeling,
linen shades half
drawn, porch steps rotted.

We step carefully
over bleached ground,
lizards skitter underfoot.

The front knob turns.
We find a mildewed foyer—
stairs leading down
too spidery to chance—
step past a tiny room,
a closet, a shelf
empty of everything.

Another room, big
as a ballroom—we peruse
the residue: hand-built benches,
a stage; mahogany walls
paneled tongue and groove.

Upright a piano, which tuned
to an evangelical hymn or
shook burlesque. No way to tell
whether the residents raised corn
or hell. A house foreclosed
speechless as a pine box.

Wild Museums

What looks very old might have happened
just yesterday, though no calendar exists
at the fossil beds of western Nebraska,
where cute pony-sized rhinoceroses
from Asia met native-born cousins
22 million years ago, probably in July,
long summer nights conducive to rhino raves
and sex swaps. The remains
(sharp footed, skull heavy) show
signs of heavy dancing in the rain.

The rancher who found the bones entertains
one of the late Crazy Horse's sisters, who adds
to the collection, giving him the chief's last
possession, a whetstone. There it is
in the museum next to the skeletons,
an artifact of Lakota history, slightly shy
of the age of granite.

Not that far away, inside Jim Gatchell's Museum
in Buffalo, Wyoming, a stylish woman,
Mrs. Jack Weldrum, as her name lives in local history,
parades in a long dress under a black parasol
along Main Street during the Diamond Jubilee
of statehood, Fourth of July weekend, 1959,
the same day Irine Humphrey & Lou Percell
pose under the sign

                ELECTRIC SUPPLIES

two old birds whose batteries surely have run down.
The faded color Kodak verifies their mortal existence,
reminds us the Wild West is long gone.

Little Big Horn

> "The Great Spirit gave us this country
> as a home. You had yours."
>
> Crazy Horse (Lakota)

Strewn like wild flowers, granite rock roots
on the withered crest, slabs of marble
summoning pilgrims to the shrine.

> A'KAVEHE ONAHE
> LIMBER BONES
> A CHEYENNE WARRIOR
> FELL HERE ON
> JUNE 25, 1876
> WHILE DEFENDING
> THE CHEYENNE
> WAY OF LIFE

Gray men, war buffs, preach to the boys,
pointing to the ravines of famous errors,
miscalculations, blind spots on the ridge,
exposed flanks where the cavalry shot
horses for barricades, distance from water.

> U.S. SOLDIER
> 7TH CAVALRY
> FELL HERE
> JUNE 25, 1876

The kid knows the lessons of thirst,
he's sat four days in the back seat,
heard of Custer's initiative, bravery,
hubris. He knuckles sweat from his eyes.
What's a massacre, Dad?

Dad hesitates, thinks slit noses, scalps,
a stick pushed into each ear so those who refuse
to listen will hear better in the next world,
an arrow stuffed up the penis to teach
the General not to fuck Native women.

The spectacle, spacious as mountain vista,
too grand to absorb each little horror
the one by one killing that sickens, terrifies.
Summer sun blazes the air, dry grass drinks
the traveler's tears. He has lost his voice.

Crazy Horse Faces the Music

Low limbs of the cottonwood
call to mind the disturbance,
a distracted mother tied the rope
and hanged herself.

The warrior passing a landmark
learns to turn, to see from another angle
all sides aren't the same. He studies
the trail back; he can imagine other
ways to follow his mother home,

paints himself yellow, adds white spots;
ties a hawk feather to his hair. He knows
never to argue with a man while facing him,
but to slip behind, look with the other's eyes.
He sees Custer circle in the palm of his hand.

In victory the path eludes him. A white man
tells Crazy Horse to *face the music.*
He enters the Soldiers Village
but when he turns, a bayonet stabs his back.
It is good, some say. *He looked for death.*

Things We Missed

We didn't visit Rushmore, nor see the stone facade of Crazy Horse.

We didn't fish for trout in blue lakes
built by the Army Corps of Engineers.

We ate no buffalo steak; we ate no buffalo stew.

We didn't engage in conversation with bronze statues of the presidents
waiting at street corners for the lights to turn green.

Most things we missed because our senses tuned to vivid cliffs
and falls and fossil pits.

We missed the road sign
to the Lakota people's sacred center of the earth.

We could not glimpse,

> before railroads, strip mines, banks,
> before territory and states,

what flourished, disappeared.

Epitaph

His gifts at last received, I've found
a sacred place he described long ago.

Here on a windy hill above wide plains,
the blue-gray horizon shapes a full circle,
sun turning to evening ash. In a minute
the first star, but now the pink glows
under sooty clouds, far trees dark as ravens.

Charles King Swan—"call me Chuck":
Four decades past, the student asks
with dignity, may he correct the history
of his people, Wisconsin's Ho Chunk.

He quotes old chief Neopit, second son
of Oshkosh, *We will not consent
to the sale of any more land. . . .*
He quotes Black Elk, Oglala holy man,
Only crazy men would sell Mother Earth.

I search for the story of Ho Chunk—
find Charles King Swan on page one
in the newspaper, his obituary yellow
as summer grass. Too late to say
thanks for his timeless stories.

Dr. Chuck, I last saw happy on a bicycle.
His spirit inspires these travels. History,
myth spun tight with prairie and plains:
the importance of knowing where.

PART 2

Rio Grande

Red clay baked into ceramic, bare levees
on both shores shelter the empty land.

Nothing moves between but the drawling river
mud-creased, deep enough to swallow a man
to his hips or scuttle a raft of refugees.

I watch a gray hawk skim the mucky bed, flutter
empty-beaked into Mexico, patrol the ocotillo, circle
back to bronze dunes in the land of pecan and cotton.

The border's porous as heat but no coyote dares
sneak through the unguarded crossing before dark.

Checkpoint

Tan boots delicate as doeskin,
a chocolate finger, knuckles
smooth at the holster.
Rodriguez, reads his badge
on the gray camouflage.

Driver's license, Ma'am?
Mister, she goes,
I'm not driving.

Two cameras behind him,
his green lens reflects
two behind her. The wind lifts
black fabric, affirms the ass.
Yes. His voice continues,
scratchy, lips shut against
the blow.

Air very hot, pasty, eyes
wait two drawn seconds.
Her left heel in woven sandal
pushes back, flattening
edges of sand, holds
its position. *Come,* he says,
with me. Please.

An inconvenience,
this mistake soon will.
Here, this way. He watches
her dress, the other soldier
locks my eyes.

Desert

The desert scoffs at commodity.
My borrowed Ford strains
to defeat heat and distance, dims
the illusion of safety. A traveler's
inclined to think imprudently
how far away can rescue be?

Far: as serial killers know, steering
prey onto the dunes. Slow winds
and sun blur tire tracks, footsteps,
eventually bury bones, though four-
legged wolves often arrive first.

The desert knows its business,
how to cook a body fast, tender.
Find out, step off the blacktop.
Enter the land of enchantment.
No one else will see exactly
where you stop, when you go.
No one expects a quick return.

Hatch

Heat rises, ants crawling on skin.
Miles ago we passed gas pumps,
now only shuttered stations.
Water we forgot doesn't help.

A dry tongue sharpens one's vision
of discovery, defines the point of travel.
All roads are on earth, someone's grandmother
promised. We reconsider, keep going.

Around a curve, the crest turns white
as if snow fell in July or cotton buds burst—
soaring upward on broad wings, a swan,
two swans striking into cloudlessness.

Hallucinatory: we'll know what's real
when we get there, an oasis called Hatch
"Green Chili Capitol of the World," today
invaded by gringos passing as white birds.

16 de Septiembre Fiesta

Maybe it's the hot sun exciting
them, a dozen women in white
blouses, yellow skirts
embroidered red, wavy hair
pinned with gardenias. They start
slowly, wrists open, dancing,
their circle ever wider, approaching
our ring of watchers. Already my skin
shivers, seeing trickles of sweat
irrigating powdered faces.

She comes close, the tall one,
yellow crests swelling
from darker roots. She taps
my shoulder, invites me, old gringo,
to dance. Oh ho, struggling to my feet,
I grasp her damp hand, mimic
the flight of her steps.

Jiggles of flesh—
mine, hers—and working down
my spine, tickles
of salt. The dancing
thickens my breath. I get
a sour desire
to hawk and spit. My step
slackens, she slides away
to another dancer, a woman.
I keep some pride.

Now thirst, a little hunger oblige
me to weave across the blazing plaza.
Mulberry leaves, like hat brims against
heat, shade the way. Bare-chested
motorcycle boys outside the café hang
onto bottles of beer, swinging
little struts, flaunt muscles
and paunch. When they are gray

and achy, they'll understand
what they've wasted.
Well, tonight I'm strong enough
to drop into bed and dream,
that yellow woman
whispering in my ear
You do fine for me, Tio.
I'm aroused, no question,
but what I reply—for this
is my dream, no time
to lie, making up
pitiful stories of desire—
I can't even do fine for myself.

Crossing the Black Range

In treeless foothills, where pioneers rushed in
—and out: in the ruins of imploded pine cabins,
fallen fence, the sag of tin and heavy labor,
spiny ocotillo roots in bare gardens.

The road rises toward grave clouds shadowing
thick juniper, piñon, Ponderosa pine; rock shelves
spill yellow stones as the lanes switch back, go up.
Nothing approaches; nothing follows. I stop.

A lean, thick-pelted dog trots out of nowhere, glances,
disappears; then a ten-prong stag shows at the edge,
stands. Such perilous potential, I greet the cold crest:
fifty, eighty mile vista, broad-winged hawks circling.

Ominous comes to mind when the wolf-dog returns:
I back my way to the car, slip inside, slowly roll
down the thicketed ridge, the road rimmed
by spires of red rock, yellowing aspen, skittish birds.

Darkness afflicts an old man's journey, this last day
of summer; lonely, constant. Riding the brakes past
charred forest, black stumps and trunks, flattening
into hazy tranquility: too late now to stake a claim.

Waiting for the Moon

Sun broils the plaza. I loiter
over cheese tortillas, lukewarm beer,
waiting for a pink flare to awaken
stone mountains across the desert.

Time then to enter shaman country—
gypsum dunes white as snowfall,
wilderness of yucca and violet roses
bedded on crests slippery as the sea.

The full moon's expected, first
night after the longest day. How
the ancients marked this celestial
coincidence is lost. I'm on my own.

The sky blackens slowly, Venus appears,
red tinge of Mars, faint constellations.
Luminescent soil defines Earth's edge,
traces the orbit. My instinct's to grasp a rail.

Stiff winds chatter the dry branches.
A boy on another hill rattles a drum,
stops abruptly. A motor breaks the quiet.
Red tail lights fade into darkness.

Wind behind me slackens, night falters.
I turn east, hoping not to be fooled
by the fluorescent glare lifting
off the flats of Alamogordo.

Suddenly that red breath—the moon
igniting the desert turns my body
to ice, seeing in clean light
the vast loneliness coming closer.

Gila Canyon

A walker must improvise to gain the heights,
starting west, circling east, always up, up—

in ancient days someone dropped a rope ladder,
pulled it back when you reached the caves.

Inside, everything in the world seems below,
crescent aperture framed by mountain green.

The angle shows the path of elk, deer, grizzlies,
or unexpected traders, bands of warriors.

Lookouts observe the swerve of hawks,
never knowing what the trail may carry.

Around Ponderosa fires, 5000 years of velvet
soot, feet pounded adobe, hands drumming.

Everyone is cousin and kin, cultivates
the "three sisters": corn, beans, squash.

Yucca, prickly pear gave away their anatomies;
a scarlet Macaw, roped, flew through flames.

Then, the river dried—fish stopped—deer ran off.

A desperate people did what they'd always done—
looked to the sky, moved the fire closer to the sun.

Ash settles in the fire pits, the lint of red pigment
sticks to a stone wall—the only remains.

Journey of the Dead

> "In the name of the most holy Trinity...
> and the most Christian king
> I take all jurisdiction...from the edge
> of the mountains to the stones and sand
> in the rivers—and the leaves of the trees."
> Juan de Ornate (1598)

1

Beyond El Rio Grande, a desert trail,
the sky is fire, sand needles the skin.
A mule stumbles dead; the priest walks,
one eye blurs, one shuts completely.

White-lipped padres burst into Pueblo shade,
fingers shaping the cross, slake their thirst
for souls by chopping off black braids
snaking down the necks of Piro women.

It is the will, the work must be done: Smother
the smoky kiva with sand, shatter the clay
mask clinging to the face of the Corn Mother,
break the prayer sticks, dangerous as ghosts.

They stop in mid-stroke the Pueblo way
of intercourse: women on all fours,
men behind; their blasphemous laughter
when Spaniards ride them breast to breast.

They make the day orderly by ringing bells
or by whipping; replace the devil's circles
with right-angle adobe, install doors and locks,
expect polished silver, immaculate floors.

To eradicate error, to enforce God's will:
they rope witches around the neck, amputate
at the ankle of rebel infidels the left foot,
whip truth into the skin of dark children.

2

The Corn Mother sings to her seeds, calling
children to bring her back through the navel
of the world; she promises babies and rain—
calabash, bundles of cotton, maize.

A shaman Popé listens to two tongues: Pueblo
and Spanish, hears sonorous voices of loss,
hears the priests' talk, their purpose, application;
enemies he knows: catechism, vestment, cross.

Popé strikes with violence clear as syllogism:
at Jeméz, the rebels humor Padre Juan de Jesús,
invite him to be knighted; instead he's stripped
naked to ride on a pig, lashed, ridden himself.

Happy rebels jump into the river, rubbing soap
on their foreheads, scouring baptism; burning
confessionals, altars, images of Virgin Mary;
shit in the chalice while chanting Latin verse.

They jeer from the hills as Spaniards flee
into the desert, nine scorched and crazy days,
hearing the devil laugh; half a thousand die.
Maps brand the trail: *Jornada del Muerto.*

Trinity, New Mexico

> "Batter my heart, three-person'd God…"
> John Donne

1

April dawn, a hazy half moon blurs the canvas sky.
In spindly branches, hidden song birds waken the sun.
The road runs north toward Trinity. Dry winds rustle
mesquite, yellow creosote swells like desert waves.

Inside the gates, no shadow darkens the plain, yucca
stretches high. Powdery dust daubs my shoes gray.
My breath becomes shallow as at a grave. Voices
drop to whisper. Yellow radiation signs—creepy.

Pinned to barbed wire, reminders of wartime duty,
hurry and wait: photos of soldiers lined outside
a canteen, the Los Alamos polo team on horseback,
Oppenheimer studies the vaporized bomb tower.

A pocked steel shell, code-named Jumbo, 200-ton
encasement built to blunt a plutonium bomb,
lies next to a caption, "shipped by rail from Ohio
to a siding called Popé."

A mockup of Fat Man, tested here, proved at Nagasaki,
lazes on a flatbed truck. Boys climb up, mugging
for snapshots. A tourist, just come from Pearl Harbor,
announces she's here "rounding the circle."

2

I see my mother weeping, gift box open on her lap.
My father's in khaki, an Army airfield, shipping out
to an unnamed Pacific island. He's sent a photo,
a bracelet of colored stones. I'm the baby, confused.

3

What was that? the blind woman exclaims, 50 miles
from test site Trinity, 5:29 AM. The Gadget's fired,
propelling light through optic darkness.
I am become Death, the destroyer of worlds.

Dust clouds swirl seven miles through purple sky
shimmer the scalding desert, Jornada del Muerto.
Sand boils, bubbles into glass, mildly radioactive.
Now we are all sons of bitches, quips a scientist.

4

Late afternoon in my childhood, kitchen jittery.
Mother's penciling to my father, suddenly she looks up
at the radio: a voice crackles "power of the universe."
The war is over, she writes. *What should I make for supper?*

5

Visitors at Trinity nervous in their cars, popping soda cans.
A family of five methodically works out the number
of backpacks, caps. The mother remembers she's forgotten
her sunglasses, goes back: hesitation, stalling the moment.

Dead center, ground zero, twelve-foot lava-rock obelisk:
Phone cameras talk to each other, tourists touching
the rough sides widen their smiles. Kilroy was here.
Even the children quiet, though no one died at Trinity.

Dawn

> "We were still talking in whispers when the
> cloud…was struck by the rising sunlight."
> Joan Hinton (1921-2010)

Joan's the prodigy, though wise guys
at Los Alamos talk about her eyes.
She's not exactly young (cute 20s),
old enough to risk a chance.

She gets a girl friend to come along.
They swipe a motorbike, sneak
past yellow signs, KEEP OUT:
Will plutonium really explode?

Knees in dust, hearts in their throats,
they duck behind a sandy crest.
Joan's not sure what they're testing—
a theory? a weapon?—or why. Then

heat, fifty times the flush of shame,
a fierce white light, brighter than—
pure purple glow—unveiling up-
sweeps of wind, air sucking dust—

Wonder, the long wonder: her eyes
ravished, she can't guess what now
will follow. The unimaginable news
comes from Japan. Her heart falls.

She backtracks into the desert, hoping
science is antidote to science, collects
hot mutant pebbles, her radioactive
warnings, mails them to politicians.

No one answers. Joan disappears,
takes her brains to faraway China,
the engineer of a milk processing plant—
a woman struck by the rising sunlight.

How The World Ends

Facsimile of the first atom bombs
(*Little Boy, Fat Man)*, aerial photos
of Hiroshima, a letter from Einstein;
all I want is to get my kids outside.

I set them loose in the high-walled canyon
where a rock face narrows, shadowing
a honeycomb of stone ruins, circles laid
by ancient ones who lived before bombs.

Inside the dark kiva, the soil's redolent
of ash and urine, the children show interest
only in the ladder that leads up and out—
race to the cliffs to see faded cave drawings.

They disappeared, I explain; no one knows
what they did or said, how they drew—
or why they departed this safe valley
with corn, beans, water, animals to hunt.

The children know how a household dies,
seemingly without cause, but they play along:
Did the mountain lion die? Did fish change color?
Did the dad run away? Did the mom say, get lost?

And I laugh with them because they're cute,
clever beyond their years; because I want
to distract them from tragedy surrounding us.
What's coming they'll see soon enough.

PART 3

Soundings

We're taping sound waves at Waikiki,
catch the hiss of sharp winds whipping spray;
white crinoline running in, clap and roll,
slap on the black shore.

When it's done, we'll play the sea
on the radio, accompany a true story,
fifteen seconds, maybe twice
as a requiem opens and closes
the gates of paradise.

The drone of an airplane intercedes.

Beginnings are always uncertain.

We wait for the ripples to settle
and lose the call of a passing gull.

We wait for its mate. The sky
stops shivering, the director shrugs.

We wait for the woman in the parking lot
to slam the door, her chatter continues
down the beach.

A second bird, a third refuse to speak.

Forget the bird, the director calls.
Ready: The waves comply,
lash the jetty, the struggling shore.

Breakers snap like timpani.
Foam knocks the loose rock,
stops—pebbles sigh retreat.

Cut!

Endings are never so neat.
Yesterday a rogue wave swamped
the crew, a man sank without a sound.

Pearl Haiku

> "You cannot escape anxiety, you
> cannot escape a clutch of fear."
> Eleanor Roosevelt (7 December 1941)

1

Sleepy green island,
breeze swaying coconut trees,
fragrant gardenias.

Edge of wet winter,
rising sun ignites the day,
sizzles sky, sea, flesh.

2

School boys played a game
we named Day of Infamy:
we yelled *Sneak Attack!*

pushed over the chairs,
Japped out cry-baby victims
grabbed their testicles.

3

An oblong casket,
Arizona's rusted hull
catacomb of bones.

Oil still swims up drop
by brown drop, skating smoothly
on the salt surface.

Iridescent stains
float farewell, coded warnings:
waves refusing sleep.

Panama Hotel, Seattle

> "War with Japan will be no pink tea."
> Senator Monrad Wallgren (7 December 1941)

1

News flash interrupts
The Great Gildersleeve, all day
stare at radio.

Cold darkening skies,
window shades drawn for blackout,
children hushed, tea steeps.

No sleep, then door knocks:
FBI shouts, grabbing books,
Japanese Bibles.

Apologizing,
Issei Grandpa holds his hat,
they take him away.

2

Japanese may bring
only what you can carry:
cups, teapot, baby.

Dog left with neighbors,
household goods stored at hotel;
owners don't return.

Ghosts alive in trunks:
bride's veil, wristwatch, laced ice skates,
her orange-checked blouse.

Tule Lake

1

Past pine and fir, mists drift
like cotton wool
below snowy crests, the train
crawls into the cold desert.

Dry lakebed bristles with black pebbles,
tiny fossil shells,
boys nicking knees on shards.
A stinging wind squints the eyes.

Mothers clutch children, bags
of clothing; fathers teeth-clenched,
hurry into brown raw-board barracks.
No glimpse of mountains over wire.

Long hours to look at walls,
waiting in lines at latrines,
shamed bodies angle away. The open
knot-hole affronts ear and eye.

2

Scrawls of Japanese characters slide down
the water-stained dormitory wall, each visitor
offers a different translation. Today's youth
remote from old world language—or maybe
a random spray of bird shit conceals the key.

One Nisei scribbles parallel English letters,
```
        *       A
        *       M
        *       ER
        *       IC
        *       A
```

I'd guess the marks mean SCREW!

3

Concrete slab overrun by sagebrush
preserves circular drain holes; toilets
without doors taught inmates the futility
of modesty, made them live in their bodies.

Remembering loss, keeping up the past—
baseball teams, newspaper stand, beauty contests,
Lucky Strikes, enamel teapots, embroidery—
telling the boy his father is away on business.

4

A steel whistle at mid-day quiets the mess.
The president sends personal greetings:
*No loyal citizen denied the democratic right
to responsibilities, regardless of ancestry...*

All relocated persons must now answer
two questions. One answer is correct:
*Are you willing to serve...combat duty?
Swear unqualified allegiance to the USA?*

Yes-Yes: 33,000 Nisei enlist to fight, join
secret intelligence, translate intercepts;
"Go For Broke" Regimental Combat Team
earns most medals, most killed, wounded.

No-No: and the boys fight on another front;
no window bares the day, no bulb may burn.
Heat from a distant stove dissolves in corridors,
the interrogation room holds two men and a bat.

Difficulty was encountered, a guard reports.
Kobayashi hit on the head…blood gushed out…
Baseball bat broke in two…I knocked my Jap
down with my fist…like shooting ducks.

5

Memoirs they will write:

> *War Without Mercy*
> *Years of Infamy*
> *Though I Be Crushed*
> *Lost Years*
> *Through Innocent Eyes*
> *A Fence Away from Freedom*
> *Betrayed*
> *Uprooted*
> *Impounded*
> *Too Long Silent*

6

The west wind shivers my leather jacket,
clumps of sagebrush bound like hurdlers.
"So muddy in winter they had to build catwalks."
On a concrete wall, penciled verse pleads:

When the golden sun has sunken beyond
the desert horizon and darkness follows
under a dim light casting [on] my lonesome heart.
Show me the way to go home.

Loss

For John Okada (1923-1971)

> "The lieutenant listened and he didn't believe it:
> He said: 'That's funny. Now tell me again.'
> The Japanese-American soldier told it again...
> 'They could kiss my ass,' said the lieutenant
> from Nebraska."
> John Okada, *No-No Boy* (1957)

He came home from war
not to boast about medals
earned in blood
while his folks were impounded
or how Japanese GIs
freed Jews at Dachau.

He knew how many died
at Salerno, Monte Cassino,
Anzio, Bruyères, the Vosges;
he knew their motto,
Go For Broke and why.
"I have my reasons," he said.

And depicted the principled
ones who answered the inquisition
positively—
No and No
knowing they were right,
history showed.

Wrote them into blank pages
no reviewer praised
no editor wanted a second look.
Such unrequited love
and loss, the widow burned
an entire book.

Confinement

> "And always my vision and my thoughts were drawn to Castle Rock, comparing our fate to the Modoc Indians' last stand in their Lava Bed Campaign of 1872-73."
> Violet Kazue de Cristoforo (Japanese American, Tule Lake inmate)

Exiled Japanese
face the fate of Modoc tribe,
caged behind barbed wire.

Nisei know Modoc
starved on nearby Castle Rock,
chiefs captured, then hanged.

Lonely days in camp
staring at lava beds: *How
abandoned I felt!*

Years dried in desert,
the poet swallowing tears,
haiku terse, salty.

Japanese can't see
old Modoc wall writing but
both sang forlorn tunes:

*I, the song, walk here.
I the dog stray in the wind.
A bad song I am.*

PART 4

Contact

From the Journal
of Father Pedro Font
31 March 1776

We came upon a poor Indian

carrying a bunch of grass.

But as soon as he saw us

he showed
the greatest possible fright

it is possible to describe.

He could do nothing

but throw himself
full length,

hiding in the grass,
raising his head

only

to peep at us with one eye.

Almost without speaking,

he offered his bunch of grass,

as if with the present

he hoped

to save his life.

He must never have seen

Spaniards before,

we caused him

such surprise and fear.

Fort Ross

Harsh winds blow across abandoned
graves, my feet catch sea vibrations
below. Redwood crosses hover
like lightning-struck stumps, names
scoured by centuries' storms.

White trawler coming in, seals
barking for supper; an orange sun
shadows humpback whales. I watch
for the spray. A woman sights
through a lens, pointing at the horizon.
We look all day, never see a sea otter.

Waters once otter-rich shimmer
in August light. A single sailboat bobs
in the blue bay, no sound reaches
this height. Only ruins remain
where Russians and Aleut prayed,
crafted homes, carved glass windows
to face the violent sea.

Wandering above shroud and skeleton,
I hear their murmurings
underfoot, lonely adventurers
forever homeless, forgotten, unknown.

Our Silence

In rainy woods, the teacher passes around
a musket, lets the boys heft its weight,
shows the girls how to pour powder. A shot
breaks the silence, chases a single black bird.

Pretend we aren't here, he says: the spruce
darker, nests alive; beaten paths uncleared.
Pretend the river named for Lewis & Clark
has kept its course, freshens fox, bear, elk.

Pretend the groan of engines, rumble of cars,
echo the sounds of rocky falls upstream;
the men fishing cross creeks and rivers
on the backs of a million silver salmon.

Suppose it's true, native Chinooks are extinct—
Clapsops, Chehalis, Qwatsamts vanished.
A squirrel chatters, ravens croak, butterflies
tease the buds. Who will tell our stories?

Restless Spring

The land's restless, so much rain
these last weeks, oaks toppling.
Red dirt crumbles to the roadside.
Pacific winds shake the stiff pines.

Melt and flood; dams open, giving
salmon a run for the homecoming.
The blue jays are back, lilacs ripen.
Is that Whitman keening on the porch?

In the side yard I hear collisions:
bees, hummingbirds, lemon buds.
Spring is so deceptive. After the cat
ran off, all I found were blue feathers.

Redwood

Transcontinental I fly thousands of miles.
The redwood in my yard merely glances
at silver airplanes sailing over its crest—
though I think long about the shadow it casts.

I would take the redwood along, if I could,
but I'd still miss the proud blue jay winging
late in the afternoon to the pinnacle,
pronouncing claim to the Pacific vista.

I return to the redwood as a cheating lover
enters the house with roses, confessing all
the reasons for disloyalty: the chance to help
a stranded refugee, to make this world better.

The redwood pays no attention as it pays no
taxes or rent for its roots, nor sobs about men
driven mad by torture. Outrage is the human
scent. I explain this to my redwood, to no end.

This Curve of Earth

Outside the kitchen window,
fence boards groan, termites
play with their breakfast.

On the stakes, black squirrels rush
in busy columns, collide, leapfrog
the rules of trespass, tariffs,

border ethics, loyal to neither side.
They nullify the neighbor's spite fence
encroaching on my land.

After noon, blue jays come yelling,
attack the scarlet tomatoes glazed
in sunshine on the pickets, temptations

I resist until the neighbor goes to Vegas.
At sunset, skunks parade, nosing
into scents buried centuries

before my neighbor cemented the posts,
drew a line hard as a territorial treaty. Nightfall,
raccoons claw through the cans, curtains

for a slow mouse. Opossums arrive late,
stay longest: burrow beneath the boundary,
promote free trade, immigration, peace.

By midnight, as a hard wind thumps
the brittle wood, dark-haired coyotes smuggle
frightened refugees through the cracks. I'm inclined

to predict an avenging disaster—earthquake,
wildfire—come to throttle my neighbor's affront
to this curve of Earth.

Underground

My ear presses earth, a lyric
spring gurgles in the hollows
of withered roots, the tallest redwood
in the county killed
by the neighbor's fondness
for concrete and brick.

I'm nostalgic for spring visits
of a rare tree-bark fly,
its niche once hidden
behind the grape roots
before the neighbor swapped
the fruit for a palisade
she says will last a hundred years.

This mountain's squeezed by city
sprawl. Trails of white-tailed deer,
skunk alleys dead end in driveways.
In darkness, only in darkness,
the animals come to speak their minds,
gobbling rose buds, toppling pails
for chicken bones, pepperoni pie.

It's heroic disobedience—roof rats
in the eaves, raccoons digging deep.
The creek has re-occupied its buried bed,
waits for a chance to toss the covers.

I bide my time, as the owl watches
for the mouse's move—a temblor, say,
earth asserting its realm: tectonic plates
snap, roads buckle, pipes burst, the house
next door stumbles drunkenly away.
The rivers shake with laughter.

After the Storm

The ocean's done its heavy lifting,
brought in the lumber and bottles,
a broken sailboat rudder, the bottom
of a bikini. Now the gleaners come,
picking driftwood, seashells, kelp.

This labor I know because two sturdy-backed glaziers
puttied weatherproof panes in a beachside diner,
revealing multitudinous coastal Californians
at work: gray-coated, the gulls trawl for lunch,
a hundred-wheeler humpback hauls
cargo down the old Pacific highway.
Thundering whitecaps beat against sand,
pound the rhythm of a tectonic tune. Not an eye
muscle relaxes. Work, work, I watch all day.

The Window

It's exhausting to watch a body die,
not a minute released, not a new idea.

Eyes on the window, her mind stayed clear
and sad, her sorrow deeper than ours.

The breaking waves outside beat
with such constancy—

        swell, white cap, crash, running surf;
        swell, white cap, crash—

The children rehearse something
they're too numb or shamed to say.

What the waters take and obscure.

Boys in black-skin suits ride the crests,
swim back, jockey, tip.

The rhythm's easier there, more paced than
on land where remorse and fear interrupt.

See how the surfer perches, floods to shore,
reverses, never dares the open sea.

Winter Light

The bridge will be scuttled
for a modern span, spilling new light
on the tides roiling the bay.
Before opportunity is forever lost,
I enter the island shore, stone jetties facing
the hard current, late sun, clouds smoldering
like charcoal. A hundred geese soar north
running before the storm.

Curls of water rise like strands of carpet,
eyelets for fish to peek at the molten sky,
for gulls to track their meals.
A bird strikes, silver prey breaks
the filmy surface. A woman anchored
on the jetty snaps her shot.

In short days of winter, the eye strains
to see further, earth's elements converge
without purpose, continuing after
witness ceases, after the eye opens
in darkness beyond the bridge.

PART 5

Appalachia

The man at the river
with watery blue eyes tells
me how to find everything
he's lost. Scratchy voiced, pointing
a crusty finger
like a needle knitting
through thickets,
he weaves the route:

First to Cousin Jack's barn,
near the yard where the collie sleeps
and across a narrow bridge
by the broken white fence
where Dave's truck flew off
leaving his Jeannie
and the two baby girls. Turn
at the gray-stone post office.
Can't miss it. Just opposite
Frank's busted Ford that needs a motor,
he's waiting for the government check.
Now if you see the church, fresh-
painted white, you've gone too far.
Turn back in Sharon's drive,
she don't ever mind, her boys
left these parts years ago.

Stories hang here, ghost-sheets
over the depleted woods. I stop
in a clearing to look at leaves fluttering,
swirling off sycamore, hickory, oak—
the way a child turns back to wave—
the mountain stripped at the ridge.

Ponds

Shimmering light edges the emerald
pastures, ponds carved into the corners
of grass fields when highways went in:
cheap landfill for road grades, cash
for farmers, bonanzas for ducks,
Canada geese, meandering goldfish.

Lightning bugs grasped in children's hands,
mosquitoes squashed on skin—otherwise
little news to report without the thumbprint
of ponds, only cows and the stout woman
with her milk pail turning toward
the glare, reflections never seen before.

Wheeling, Dealing

Gone are the smoky mills, dust
of big-wheeled coal trucks dropping
rock down waterfront slides. Rusty
river bins have sunk or floated away.

*

Here's where the country stops,
terminus of the first National Road
hewn through hickory forest to speed
pigs and corn to market. Farmers toss
barrels of mash whiskey from wagon
to flat boat, paddle down the blue Ohio.

Here city speculators pick coffles
of chattel, Virginia boys and girls,
chain field hands to cart wheels,
ship them to auction in Natchez
or a sporting house in cotton ports.

Here America's first wire-cable
suspension attaches plantation
to prairie, speeds truant slaves running
north, helps slave catchers
dragging them back.

Here coal barons trade futures in ore,
sell bituminous stone to fire locomotives,
steamships, to heat New York hotels.

Wheeling's at the verge of the world.

*

Bygone business seeps through faded paint:
Rogers Fireproof Hotel, one-night stand
for drummers and coal dealers, defunct
as the biscuit factory, once famous for

pennant crackers and cakes. Muriel's
STOGIES shut, workers' bars dark all day.

Coal landings at the river whispering
steam, we pass yellow brick stacks
and streets of Legionnaires—
in every button hole, a flag pinned.
Inflatable rubber bunnies, drunk
in the wind, await the Easter parade.

Jim and I catch the mood, order bowls
of chili homemade in a kitchen named
for Sally. She's all chatter, pours sour
coffee, calls me "Hon." Her menu
says, *Live as if heaven is on earth.*

The Puzzle

Who'd move 60,000 tons of earth,
3 million basket loads by hand?

Emerald green, the cone-shaped mound
stands 70-feet high, 100-yards across the base,
circled by a moat, 40-feet wide.

White settlers thought
no savage Mingo
or Shawnee had the capacity,
doubted heathen could be more strenuously
religious than church-builders who pray indoors.

Jealously curious, diggers lift
pick and shovel, slit trenches,
tunnel for buried treasure.

Bones are what they find, skeletons
clad in elm bark, laid on white ash,
aligned symmetrically to sun or star,

bodies planted with copper gifts
mined from quarries at the Great Lakes,
shells sent from the southern Gulf.

Artifacts prove the devil's work
to those who see no spirits
in Appalachia's forests,
only farm, crop, harvest.

City on a Hill

> "To begin right, there will be no wrong habits to combat...no rubbish to remove before you lay the foundation."
>   Manasseh Cutler (Marietta, Ohio, 1787)

The town plan fits on a linen square:
house-lot grids, brick-paved streets.
A clerk sketches the church steeple,
marks trees, school house, city hall.

Where two rivers meet—Muskingum,
the Ohio, two inky lines on a blank
map—the planners don't know
which way the soil slopes or rolls,

only they hold an idea of wilderness,
which is neither garden nor pasture,
nor paradise but ambitious men crave
to make it home, crying Westward, Ho!

The promising land surprises them.
Someone's been here before, left
a pile of dirt a million feet square—
moat, earthen walls, ramps to the river.

Settlers vow to improve the un-virgin land,
bring orchard trees, bulls and cows, erect
walls against Shawnee, Mingo, Algonquian;
destroy palisades they can't understand.

The ancient tomb's unmovable, fills
the village center; in time entombs
the pioneers; their graves abound, oblige
their sons to worship heathen ground.

The Mountain Top

Kayford, West Virginia

The mountain man points across a half-mile gap
to a hill where silver leaves shiver in strong gusts,
to family graves, centuries old, unreachable
without permission from the coal company.

Coal keeps the lights on, the company brags.
On in the funeral parlor, the mountain man says,
inviting Jim and me to visit what's left of his hill
since the last dragline shovel devoured Appalachia.

Face smudged, boots soaked in sludge,
the old coal miner still hoists hammer
and pick to a rocky ledge, sets charges,
chokes on dust, coughs blood, dies hard.

And now comes the behemoth, ten stories high
with a button's push swallows the mountain,
each bite 50,000 tons of sandstone and root,
heaves its maw into the hollows below.

Soil, forest, whatever's above the black seams,
the company calls waste or *overburden*.
Inside the shovel the word is *spoil*, and once
the river's sunk, fish killed, they speak of *fill*.

Taking the miner out of mining means 8 billion
pounds of explosives; 800 million acres
of forest; 500 mountains collapsed—leaves
fresh yellow-painted signs saying HAZARD

    DO NOT EAT BASS
    BEYOND THIS POINT

*

We take the risky ride over washed-out gravel.
Dark leaf canopy, walls of sheer rock shadow
the way. Mud ditches raise the peril, coal
trucks racing down, hogging the road.

At the sunny crest, the mountain man guides us
past a yellow crack the size of a barbeque pit.
He calls it land rupture; I lean over to see where
it leads—down, down, a ragged black shaft.

Dynamite's ripped open the belly, gutted the hill
from below. He says, please be careful, you don't
want to fall in. We walk on toes by spindly trees
until the light opens to face the stark precipice.

The mountain next door has vanished, dropped
into the planet's bowel, an entire forest gone.
A few hawks fly around aimlessly; the wind
carries the insistent whine of motors nearby.

At the brink stands one ghost tree, black roots
sinewy, naked in mid-air, branches stiff as bone.
The mountain man studies the bark. Don't fall,
he advises. No one will come to save you either.

Twenty-Nine Dead

Just seemed like a normal day, says a miner
at the sweltering Upper Big Branch shaft,
It felt like you were melting.

Man, they got us up there mining, a digger
warns, *and we ain't got no air. I'm scared
to death to go to work...something bad.*

Today, a schoolboy's drawn a crayon picture—
In Loving Memory to the Fallen Miners—
leaves it at the statue outside the Capitol

where the bronze coal miner, lantern on his skull,
presides; his pride implied, his labor
helped build...the greatest country on earth.

The boy places a toy tractor inside a plastic bag,
gifting his cousin, as if this talisman offers
air and light to a man suffocated underground.

Profoundly reckless...corporate risk taking
the official report concludes—tribute
to faulty switches, broken gauges, neglect.

We want cheap energy, the company scoffs,
claims the blast was "an act of God," much like
the light rain washing away the boy's crayon.

Small Business

A porch of puppies for sale,
birdhouses, hand-made arrows
lead to the taxidermist.

A chainsaw drones.

Mix and make do
or shovel coal into gondolas,
pull three hundred cars east to Norfolk,
sail with the ore to Johannesburg.

Maybe ferment green kernels in deep woods,
barrel at night, disregard steeples
peeking through bare trees,
the church warning
      GIVE SATAN AN INCH
      HE WILL BE THE RULER

For a quicker buck, they sell crack.

Hidden Valley

From the trailer's open window
a flag flutters Confederate Stars,
lawn signs offer the usual array,
BATTERIES*MANURE*FRESH HONEY.

Bible signs need no text, just footnotes
(John 3:16). GOD IS GOOD quotes
a billboard, the creator of the universe
cleverly blocking our view of His wares.

Names

Names bleed through dusty brick.

    HEN & BEN
    THE SHOE MEN

MARTING'S DEPARTMENT STORE
    Here for you yesterday
    Here for you today

And gone last week. Names
that ran the river towns,
half a block from the railroad,
half a mile from home on the hill,
from Friday nights at the high school game,
Tuesdays with the Lions Club,
Elks, Legionnaires.

Ingram's towboat navigates the river,
pushing sand, gravel, rusty iron
under the dilapidated bridge.

Across the stream, two hundred-
gondola coal trains heave
slowly and forever, rattling
back windows, rocking cribs.

Main Street's quiet. Names retired.
Below faded letters LEWIS FURNITURE
glossy script announces
    ELITE INSTITUTE
    OF COSMETOLOGY.
Tone & Tanning, NAILS.
Walk-Ins Welcome.

Windows in deserted shops post
names of jobless girls who stuck around,
got pregnant, chilled on pills, fell in
and out of love, and too young died.

Street lights down, the moon still
shadows a skyline of steeples darkening
in green glare of neon TATTOO,
make-up joints, the risky fix.

Everlasting

Blue smoke hangs like mist
over two frizzy-haired women sitting
cross-legged, backs against
a brick wall, savoring morning cigarettes.

Inside, chickens have been hacked; thighs,
breasts, backs weighed and wrapped in plastic.
A young mother rolls a cart past apple sauce,
ladies stopping to cluck at her four-day son.
The butcher wipes red hands on his apron.

This isn't a tourist town, no place to eat
or sit down. Who but townspeople read
the weathered plaques on picket fences,
detailed ancestry of the yellow-frame home
of a newspaper editor dead over a hundred years,
the ex-mayor's two-story, a pool room that gave
refuge during a flood in the last century.

At the courthouse, a column honors Civil War dead.

THE ONLY UNION MONUMENT SOUTH OF THE MASON-
DIXON LINE ERECTED BY PUBLIC SUBSCRIPTION
EXCEPT THOSE IN CEMETERIES

Deeper in the etched script, a stormy history sleeps:

The War for the Union Was Right, Everlastingly Right,
and the War Against the Union Was Wrong, Everlastingly Wrong.

Such fervor—and down the block, the two women stand up,
flip away their cold smokes, oblivious

of the gray Ohio River a hundred yards away
of a tugboat stubbornly pushing against the stream
on waters that once separated slave from free.

Trespass

Spring wrens twitching
sycamore leaves, dart
from pastel green
to pair in open air.

The Ohio River bends
soundlessly,
a tall chimney bares
its orange flame.

The road winds
to a trespass warning;
a man with a cigarette
demands the car's retreat.

Conciliatory,
he doesn't say outright
he owns
the river's edge.

Off the River

Dead End, the sign is bullet pocked. We turn
in circles, but the winding river's drifted away.

A tall gray-haired woman in blue jeans hosing
her Ford pickup can't believe we're really lost.

In her garden, the Ten Commandments stand
like a row of grave stones. She gives directions.

Miles later, at the second fork, a lone farmer rakes
leaves into a fire; he points us to the highway.

Horses, sorghum, clover—the land's so various,
and every house, barn, church repeats like mailboxes.

Inside the cool Hoosier Tavern, we meet a work crew,
steak sandwiches, beer glasses in hand; the voices drop.

Indiana's low rolling hills, my father's dream—
he'd seen once from a train window during the war.

Illinois Central

Red lights, bells. White gate drops.

We've already crossed the track, stepped onto the quaky siding;
we could go on for the glass of beer, but stand to wonder.

A girl nearby is counting cars.

*Remembering: when I fell asleep on the hard cane seat, awakened
just before the station, thrilled by the first step into fresh snow*

I watch the freight—timber bark fluttering in speed;
gondolas of red sand; a line of silver tankers; skids of wood
plank; cattle cars that stink; crates of potatoes; pigs in cages.

Military jeeps covered in green tarp ride like the robed chiefs
of staff on top of the double-decker.

*the ride to Narragansett, same name at every stop until I learned
it was nowhere but a placard for a brand of beer*

Car by car, sunrise to moon, hours pass from planting to harvest,
screw to carburetor to Diesel machine.

Each car five seconds.

*on the Milwaukee Road passing by the open window, pink walls behind,
I saw the room from which I'd once watched the gray trains go by*

The steel clicks, cargo shudders, too much clatter to talk.

Endnotes

Horse Creek, 1846: See Francis Parkman, *The Oregon Trail* (1847), p. 82.

A Skirmish in the Territory, 1854: The skirmish is described in Kingsley M. Bray, *Crazy Horse: A Lakota Life* (2006), pp. 31-32.

Bugle, 1866: Adolph Metzger's battered bugle sits in a case at the Jim Gatchell Memorial Museum in Buffalo, Wyoming.

Winter Counts: A convenient introduction to the annual Lakota Counts can be found at the website of the Smithsonian Institution: http://wintercounts.si.edu/index.html. The italicized words come from *Black Elk Speaks: Being the Life Story of a Holy Man of the Oglala Sioux*, edited by John G. Neihardt (1932, 1961).

Crazy Horse Faces the Music: Italicized words are quoted in Kingsley M. Bray's biography of Crazy Horse.

Desert: "Land of Enchantment" is the New Mexico state motto.

16 de Septiembre Fiesta: The celebratory date of Mexican independence.

Journey of the Dead: Juan de Ornate: Spain's first colonial governor of New Mexico claimed all the territory and inhabitants for the monarchs of Spain. The best source for the Pueblo response is Ramón A. Gutiérrez, *When Jesus Came, the Corn Mothers Went Away: Marriage, Sexuality, and Power in New Mexico, 1500-1846* (1991).

Trinity, New Mexico: A detailed study can be found in Richard Rhodes's *The Making of the Atomic Bomb* (1986). The quote "now we are all sons of bitches" is attributed to test director Kenneth Bainbridge.

Dawn: Joan Hinton: See *New York Times* obituary, 11 June 2010.

Panama Hotel, Seattle: *Only what you can carry*: In February 1942, President Franklin D. Roosevelt issued executive order 9066, requiring the relocation of Japanese Americans on the west coast, regardless of whether they were citizens or not, into concentration camps. They were permitted to take "only what you can carry." In Seattle, many left their possessions in the basement of the Panama Hotel where some of their things can still be found today.

Tule Lake: Inside the concentration camps, federal officials tried to separate "loyal" Japanese Americans from "disloyal" Japanese Americans by requiring all men of military age to answer a questionnaire. The issues flared over giving unqualified allegiance to the United States at a time when most Japanese residents were denied the rights of citizenship. See Richard Drinnon, *Keeper of Concentration Camps: Dillon S. Myer and American Racism* (1987) and John Okada's exquisite novel, *No-No Boy* (1957).

Confinement: *How abandoned:* Violet Kazue de Cristoforo quoted in Lawson Fusao Inada, ed., *Only What We Could Carry* (2000), p. 328. See also the poignant poetry anthologized in *May Sky: There is Always Tomorrow,* edited by Violet Kazue de Cristoforo (1997).

Confinement: *I, the song*: A. L. Kroeber, *Handbook of the Indians of California* (1925), p. 321.

City on a Hill: The saga of white settlement at Marietta, Ohio is told by Frazer Dorian McGlinchey, "'A Superior Civilization': Appropriation, Negotiation, and Interaction in the Northwest Territory," in *The Boundaries Between Us,* edited by Daniel P. Barr (2006).

The Mountain Top: For mountain top removal, see Michael Shnayerson, *Coal River* (2008). See also Mountainkeeper.org

Twenty-Nine Dead: For the Upper Big Branch disaster report, see the following web document:
http://media.npr.org/documents/2011/may/giip-massey-report.pdf
A good summary can be found in *The New York Times* on 20 May 2011.

Acknowledgments

Special thanks to Casey FitzSimons, Esther Kamkar, Lee Rossi, and Robert Perry whose unrelenting honesty on Saturday mornings sometimes made me sad but a better poet; also to Charlotte Muse and Richard Silberg who refined my education. John T. Daniel, my long-distance critic and dear friend, shares a rare poetic wisdom I've come to rely on. Michael Batinski, ever perceptive and loyal, saw more of this work emerging than anyone else. To Jeannette Ferrary, I can offer only my heart in return.

I also acknowledge the publications below where some of these poems first appeared:

Blue Moon Literary Review, Crossing the Black Range and This Curve of Earth

Earthspeak, Stone Heads, Solstice, and Epitaph

Monterey Poetry Review, After the Storm

New Mexico Poetry Review, Gila Canyon and Journey of the Dead

Pacific Review, Things We Missed and Contact

Poetrybay, Underground

Poetry Flash, Medicine Wheel, Wyoming

Review Americana, Horse Creek, 1846

Sand Hill Review, Restless Spring

Written Rivers: A Journal of Eco-Poetics, Black Hills and The Mountain Top (At the Mountain Top)

ABOUT THE AUTHOR

Peter Neil Carroll has written about place in America both as historian and poet. His first book of poetry, *Riverborne: A Mississippi Requiem* (2008), inspired further travels around the country exploring lost landscapes and cultures from the Black Hills and New Mexico desert to the Ohio Valley. His poems have appeared in *Poetrybay, Written Rivers, Poetry Flash, Pacific Review, Sand Hill Review, Earthspeak, Review Americana, Blue Moon Literary Review, Monterey Poetry Review*, and *New Mexico Poetry Review*. He's also the author of a memoir, *Keeping Time: Memory, Nostalgia & the Art of History* (2011). He has taught creative writing at the University of San Francisco, taught history at Stanford University, hosted "Booktalk" on Pacifica Radio, and edited the *San Francisco Review of Books*. Born in New York City, he lives now in Belmont, California with the writer/photographer Jeannette Ferrary.

www.ingramcontent.com/pod-product-compliance
Lightning Source LLC
Chambersburg PA
CBHW031206090426
42736CB00009B/807